MW00877043

worthy

BELIEVE WHO
GOD SAYS
YOU ARE

REBECCA HASTINGS

Worthy: Believe Who God Says You Are

© Rebecca Hastings, 2017

ISBN: 978-1545480410

For my Grandma Joyce,
finally living in full understanding of
her worth.

" Jesus looked at them and said,
'With man this is impossible, but
with God all things are possible.'"

MATTHEW 19:26 (NIV)

Contents

INTRODUCTION

Not to be Skipped!

I'm going to let you in on a secret, well, lots of secrets actually. In these pages you will find truth and hope, but you'll also find honesty. I'll tell you things that have never left the swirling of my head. But you won't just read my stories. You'll read stories of other women, just like you and me, that have struggled to believe they are worthy.

You should also know, I don't have this all tied up in a pretty bow, shelved neatly in the "Things I've Completely Figured Out" section of my brain. I've made progress, but I also recognize that I won't be tying that bow this side of heaven. Part of this life is about working things out, and this is an area to keep working on because it matters.

When we believe what God says about us, we are free to love and be loved more fully. We are free to do more of what He calls us to because we're not trapped in our own thinking. **Believing you are worthy can change how you live your life.**

As we start today friend, let's agree on a few things.

1. **We will not do this perfectly.** I know on Day 1, it's easy to think we will. But the truth is life may happen. You may need more time to let the day's truth sink in. You may struggle to believe it and read the verse again and again. You may just lose track. Let's start right here agreeing to move forward in grace. Grace to get it wrong. Grace to not fully understand. Grace to keep going even when it looks messy. All grace.

2. **You deserve this.** It's a hard concept if you're not sure of your worth, but maybe believe me on this one? You deserve the time you spend reading these words, taking these action steps and praying these prayers. You deserve every minute friend. Trust me.

3. **Your worth matters to God.** It really does. We'll look at verses that show you how important this is to Him. He wants you to really know how He feels about you. YOU. Not everyone else. Not just the pastors and missionaries. Not just the good Christians. YOU. If it matters to God, it should matter to us.

Moving through these pages, you'll find stories and inspirational truths. But each day you'll also find The Daily Three. These are the three most life changing parts of each day of Worthy.

VERSE: a scripture to highlight exactly what God says about your worth.

ACTION STEP: something tangible for you to do or specific for you to think about.

PRAYER: the very words I prayed for myself and for you each day.

Can I encourage you to do something? Don't skip those parts. Honest. I know how easy it is to let your eyes skim a verse or prayer in a book. I know because I do it (notice I can't even use past tense here.) If you are going to skim words, skim the rest, but focus on The Daily Three.

Read that verse. Find it in your bible and highlight it. Read it in another version. Put it on a post-it to read for the day.

Do the thing you're called to in the action step. Really. Even if it's just jotting down a note about your thoughts or answering the question. Make this yours.

Pray. Really. Say it quiet or loud, in your car or on your knees. God hears us and meets us every time we talk to Him. Pray it throughout the day or add to it and make it your own. Amen?

Are you ready, friend? Are you ready to begin walking on a new path? I know the first steps are scary, but consider this book me holding your hand and walking beside you. I know you can do this. You can get to a place where you believe you are worthy.

DAY 1

The Things We Don't Deserve

I'm too big for that. The thought is as instant as recognizing the color of the dress on the hanger in front of me. It's not that they don't have my size. I can slide all the pretty, tiny, single digit dresses to the front to reach way back and find the dress.

The problem isn't about finding my size. It's that I don't believe I should wear the beautiful dress because my size disqualifies me from wearing something so bold. I let the fabric fall from my hand and sigh as I walk away to find something plain, something more appropriate for a woman in double digits.

I walk away defeated. Again. Maybe I should just leave?

I can't go there. The day at the beach sounded like so much fun, but how could I have fun when everyone around me is so much skinnier than me? I look at the bathing suit more closely.

Now, seriously, holding up that stretchy fabric I think to myself, *"That can't all be for me; this is supposed to be fitted."* Yet, I pull and tug and battle that fabric that was supposed to be stretchy and looked far too roomy into place. I quickly discover that it is, in fact, the right amount of fabric, and it is not quite as stretchy as I once thought.

And lest you think it's just about the bathing suit, consider the other factors of the beach. Moving around in said bathing suit. There are some things no one needs to see, and me bending over to adjust a towel on the sand in that horrible fabric masquerading as a bathing suit is at the top of the list.

And I'm supposed to smile and be relaxed because it is the sun and sand and surf after all.

Why would I want to go there?

Maybe it's not the beach. Maybe it's that party or a dinner or a wedding where it seems like everyone else has it all together and you just barely got your zipper up or mustered the courage to go without a date. The world is full of places we think we can't go because we're just not good enough.

I shouldn't get that. I know that's what the people around me are thinking. *Why would she order dessert? Can't she see how big she is?* If they're not thinking it, I am certainly thinking it for them. I can either enjoy it and feel guilty or go without.

Awesome.

I shouldn't go. Yes, I've always wanted to take that trip. But surely, I should wait until I've got my life more figured out, right? I shouldn't get the reward of a vacation until I am put together and deserve the beauty a vacation has to offer. Right?

How many things have I missed out on or walked away from in my life because I had associated my size, my status, or how orderly my life is with whether I was worthy of something beautiful or fun or special?

Somehow I subscribed to the notion that *the greater my mass or my chaos the less I deserved.*

So many of my choices revolved around a scale. I was looking for a value in the numbers that glared up at me from above my toes. I was looking for value in the invisible scale of how others see me. How do you measure up? The number on a scale will never represent your value.

God's love for us has no scale. It does not change when our bodies change. His love for us is full and complete, always. This is the single thing that makes us worthy.

We are so accustomed to believing lies because we've believed them for so long. They are automatic, reflexive, and we simply don't know what truth is, never mind how to believe it.

But we can start somewhere.

Verse: "For as high as the heavens are above the earth, so great is his steadfast love toward those who fear him,"
Psalm 103:11 (NIV)

Action Step: Think of something you want to do and do it for you without worrying about how big or small you are. Wear bright lipstick, buy the shirt you've wanted, take off the cover-up, go dancing, buy yourself flowers. You are worthy. Just as you are.

Prayer: Lord, thank you for loving me fully no matter what. Sometimes I don't understand that love, sometimes I don't believe that love, but I trust that you know better than me. I trust that your Words are truth and I cling to them always. Help me remember who You are and who that makes me. Amen.

DAY 2

Lies for a Lifetime

I can remember being a little girl and heading to one of Gram's meetings with her. It was always in the evening in the same generic church hall. There were chairs that were stacked neatly when no one was there and a table by the door. It was one of the few times I saw her get dressed up. Not fancy, but she definitely brought her A-game.

At that little folding table there would be two smiling women with pins on their sash, so many pins. It was like Girl Scouts, each pin representing an achievement. Only these were not skills obtained, no these achievements were measured against the far wall, on a scale.

My grandmother smiled more often than not, even at these meetings. And I do believe the premise is good, but as a little girl they represented one thing: striving. She was always striving.

Eighty-two years. That's how long she lived with feeling unworthy, unimportant, un-special, un-beautiful. A lifetime.

It isn't always with weight. We can strive to be younger, more popular, own more things, get the better job. Achievement is good, the world says, so go for more. Always go for more.

What if we need to embrace what we have before we can enjoy anything more? Maybe it's not about needing to be or do or have more. Maybe we need to see the things that perpetually push us toward more for what they are: lies.

Now, this is not about goals. We can set goals and achieve and that can be good. But when the goal becomes a carrot that keeps getting dangled just out of reach, that's not a goal, that's a tease. And when we live our life chasing the ever moving carrot, we live life in a constant state of pushing, striving, doing. And we forget what God called us to: be still.

My grandmother died a few years ago, yet the struggle in her heart still makes me sad. The consolation is knowing that she is no longer feeling unworthy. People may think that the healing she received going to heaven is about the ability to walk without pain or beating the infection. That is part of it, but the most beautiful healing she is walking in now is that of the heart.

I don't want to wait for heaven to believe I am worthy of love and joy and life. She may not have been able to do that in this world, but I can. And so can you.

A lifetime is too long to live believing a lie. When we make the choice to change we can live in a new freedom believing who God says we are.

Verse: "Then you will know the truth, and the truth will set you free." John 8:32(NIV)

Action Step: Sometimes changing the heart is difficult, but start here with me today. Remind yourself of God's truth. Write this verse out with one truth God says about you and read it a few times a day. In fact, be bold and read it out loud in front of a mirror.

Prayer: Lord, help me be brave and believe. I don't want to spend a lifetime believing all the things I'm not. I want to spend every day from this day forward believing who You say I am. I don't want to waste another day. And when those thoughts come creeping back in, help me to be brave and bring them to You. Amen.

DAY 3

How The Past Impacts Our Worth

The bus stop was the transition place in my day. It was the link between my happy, loved life at home and what was about to come as soon as I walked up those big steps. I often wondered what excuse I could make to go back in the house, back where I knew who I was.

Before I could think of a reason mom would believe, the big yellow bus pulled up, both the bus and I groaning as it came to a stop.

As the door opened I would walk closer, the only glance up was the moment I tried to meet the bus driver's eyes. The bus driver wasn't warm and had places to go, so I would look down and pull myself up the steps turning to face the endless rows of seats.

My hips seemed to touch both sides, another reminder that I wasn't like the other girls. I began to shuffle down the aisle, looking down, hoping to see an empty seat to settle into, invisible. But it never came.

"Go away skank girl."

I kept walking, never making eye contact. If I was what they said I was, what right did I have?

I walked slow, ignoring the laughter. The only saving grace to looking down was that I didn't see the faces they were making at me.

Making my way further back, my odds got less and less. I watched people move to the edge of their seat, as if the space their backpack was filling was more important than a space for me. They usually let me get all the way to the back, so I had to turn around and move toward the front again. That was when the bus driver would finally intervene with a no nonsense "Take a seat," probably watching the cars line up waiting for me to finally find a place.

Eventually, I would force myself into a seat, ignoring the groans and comments of the unlucky one who happened to be in the seat with me.

I almost felt bad for them.

I'm ashamed to even type the words. This was my reality on the bus daily as a nine year old girl. I still don't understand. I didn't really know what was wrong, but looking back I see what they saw.

I was a girl without a dad, living in a house the size of a shed. My clothes weren't new, and they certainly weren't trendy. My hair was often a tangled mess. It wasn't because I wasn't cared for, but because of what we didn't have. Even as a kid money matters more than it should. I still haven't forgotten it no matter how much I wish I could.

Do you have big steps you dreaded walking up? It may not have been the bus, but we all have a collection of yesterdays, some better than others.

Things from our past can somehow find a way to force themselves into our present. Words spoken, actions taken, and experiences had can leave scars that never seem to fully heal. Soon you can't tell the blood stains from fresh wounds.

I'm here to tell you that you don't need to hold onto it. You don't need to stare at those scars wondering when they will bleed again.

But sometimes the thoughts come on their own, don't they? The memories hitting hard with invisible fists, taking us out with ideas that we are ugly, not good enough, not worth it, too much, never changing.

When those thoughts from the past fight their way into our present we are not helpless. We have a weapon we can use.

Our only job is to take those broken, wounding thoughts captive. Grab them, recognize them and ask God to take care of them.

The past will never be as strong as our God.

If the thought does not align itself with God's truth, there is no place for it in your life.

Verse: "We use our powerful God-tools for smashing warped philosophies, tearing down barriers erected against the truth of God, fitting every loose thought and emotion and impulse into the structure of life shaped by Christ."
2 Corinthians 10:5 (MSG)

Action Step: What thoughts threaten to claw their way into your present? Take each one to Jesus and see how He will bring them into obedience.

Prayer: Jesus, you know those things from my past that invade my present. I'm so tired of them. I don't want them in my life or my thoughts anymore. I bring each one to you and I trust you to take care of it. If they come up again, I will bring it to You again and again until it is no longer a part of my life. Thank you for knowing my heart and caring for me more than I know.
Amen

DAY 4

From Generation to Generation

I look just like my mom. Seriously. The family resemblance is so strong I've had strangers in the store stop me when I'm all alone asking if I was related to her. We're often mistaken for sisters, which is fine by me as long as I'm the younger sister.

I think it's the eyes. And the hair. And the skin. In fact there's more that's the same about us than different. I like having parts of her overlap with parts of me.

So many things in us can overlap, can't they?

Her eyes, his smile, her laugh, his sense of humor.

We pass down so many things through our family lines. Looks, personality traits, likes, dislikes. It's all there.

But there's something else there, too, that gets passed down. Things that we don't take the time to notice, but that doesn't change the fact that they exist.

I look at my mom and her mom.

Like a funhouse mirror showing reflection after reflection endlessly, I see us. Three generations of women struggling with the same thing. We are great at smiling and being happy, but everything we do and everything we say and think is pulled down by an undercurrent of unworthiness. Some days are easier than others. Some days we function and laugh and go about life almost forgetting. But some days we get caught in a riptide, gasping and frantically looking around wondering how to break free.

I wonder how far back we can trace this feeling of unworthiness. But the truth is, even one generation is too far.

Whether you love your family or you are working out your past you can't erase the role they play in your beliefs about yourself. They have a large role in how worthy you feel of love and beauty and joy. It may make you feel like it's out of your control, like your hands are tied. But you have the only thing you need to be free.

We have Jesus. He can break anything that holds us back, anything in our family lines, anything that lies under the surface and wish we never inherited.

Let's take a moment today and ask God to take care of anything in our family lines that hinder us from understanding our worthiness.

Verse: "Therefore, if anyone is in Christ, he is a new creation. The old has passed away; behold, the new has come."
2 Corinthians 5:17 (ESV)

Action Step: Identify one lie from your family line or your past that you don't want to be part of your life anymore. Bring it to Jesus right now.

Prayer: Dear God, please come and remove anything from my past and my family lines that keeps me from seeing myself the way you see me. Break off any ties that hold me back, and help me live in complete freedom to receive all the good things you have for me. Let me declare boldly that I am Your new creation. Thank you God that you are bigger than any pieces of my past, and that You love me completely. Amen.

DAY 5

Mistakes

We all have them. Sometimes they are out there for the world to see and sometimes we tuck them into the crevices of our heart. But we have all made mistakes. There are things that make us wish life was a computer and we could push the undo button.

Like that time with my dad.

I was so mad. No one would listen to me. No one cared. I was spewing anger and I honestly can't even remember why. But I do remember what I did in my anger.

I swore. At my dad. The one man who has given me more than I could have imagined. It was forever ago, but in my heart I can still taste it hot on my tongue and feel the regret that followed.

I've apologized. He's forgiven me. But the past comes at us brutal sometimes and knocks us down until we're left on the floor.

This may seem small and insignificant to you. Or maybe it is unfathomable. Either way, **our mistakes are not as much about the act as how we perceive the act. That determines how deeply we hold onto it.**

Some of us may be struggling with mistakes that seem unforgivable. Things we can't even whisper in the dark. Things that haunt us and break us over and over again reminding us that we are not, nor will we ever be worthy.

Those are lies.

The past has a way of burrowing deep and making itself at home. Our mistakes feed on time and we let them fester until they are all we can see, hear, taste.

I'm a terrible daughter for swearing at my dad. You made a mistake and you are forgiven.

I'm the worst mom. I screamed at my kids. *You made a mistake and you are forgiven.*

I cheated.

I stole.

I can't even write what I did.

Yet the answer is still the same. *You made a mistake and you are forgiven.*

We believe what we feel instead of what we know.

No matter how old, bad, or secret your mistakes are, they are in the past. And they don't need to be part of your future.

When we bring the mistakes of our past to God, He doesn't forgive the way we do, with a file tucked away for later reference. No, He forgives completely, removing all traces of evidence against us. He covers it in blood and Jesus' blood is a beautiful stain to wear.

We can't fathom this type of forgiveness because it is unfathomable. It is too much. And we talk ourselves out of thinking it's for us. But God never stops. He never changes and His offer always stands.

If you are struggling with letting go of mistakes that you've made, listen carefully today and be set free.

Verse: "As far as the east is from the west, so far has he removed our transgressions from us." Psalm 103:12 (NIV)

Action Step: Write down one mistake you've been holding onto. Hold it and ask God to forgive you. Then destroy the paper.

Prayer: Thank you God that you forgive so completely. I wish I could grasp that fully, but sometimes my mistakes burrow deep into my mind and I believe their lies instead of You. Please help me to believe You and Your forgiveness. Help me let go of those mistakes that I hold so deep inside and turn them over to You with all my heart. Amen.

DAY 6

The Past Does Not Define Us

I added up time one day: 19 years. 90 days. 11 hours.

That's how long he's stayed.

7025 days that he hasn't left me.

He says he never will. He says he's in it for good. I believe him. I really do.

But there's a whisper telling me that he'll leave. And it has nothing to do with him.

The problem is that it's not what I know. My scope of experience is so far from the idea of someone staying. It only took one person to change that in me, and I sometimes wonder how many it will take to heal that place to a point of believing.

My biological father left. It happened so long ago when I was chubby cheeked and bright eyed as only a three year old can be. He was part of my life for a long time, until he wasn't. We haven't spoken in almost twelve years, and as much as I forgive there are still days when it hurts. It hurts like a scar, long ago healed, yet when you look at it you remember. Sometimes it all comes back in a rush and other times it's a quiet remember when. Either way, healed pain still leaves scars and scars still make us remember.

Do you have any scars? Maybe yours are old like mine, a memory of a pain you'd rather forget. Or maybe they're newer, still healing, still becoming part of your new skin. Either way, there is healing and there is hurt. And those two extremes can make it so hard to know love.

It's hard to believe what real love is, what it looks like when we're so very flawed.

When we live in a world of hurt and pain it's easy to think that love just isn't in the cards for us. We don an artificial bravado and toughen up to the facts. *We let our past experiences define our future worthiness.*

When we live in all of our yesterdays love becomes fuzzy. When I choose to believe my past that tells me that husbands stop loving their wives and dads leave their daughters I am believing that my history is my future. I am believing that I am not worthy of love.

Past events do not define who we are, and someone else's choices do not change our value. But we have to choose to believe that. We need to believe that sometimes there is hurt and damage, but it does not change that we were born to love and be loved. Sometimes our circumstances and experiences give love a bad name; there may have even been a song about that. But if that's the case it's not the love we were meant for anyway.

God's pure love is what we were designed for. This is what we are worthy of. We are worthy to love and to be loved. We are worthy of hope and beauty and safety in that love. Maybe if we can start believing it, we can walk in trust that God is for us, that His love is never-changing and we can live life knowing we are worthy of love.

Our scars do not define us. His love does.

Verse: "Forget the former things; do not dwell on the past. See, I am doing a new thing! Now it springs up; do you not perceive it? I am making a way in the wilderness and streams in the wasteland."
Isaiah 43:18-19 (NIV)

Action Step: What scars do you have? Are you letting them define who you are and what you are worthy of? Can you write down that scar as small as you can? It can be a word that reminds you (but make it tiny). Now, Use that as the starting point to draw something beautiful - a flower, a design, a star.

Prayer: God, help me recognize my scars for what they are, evidence of the past, without giving them power over my future. Help me find my definition of worth in who You say I am instead of giving the things that happen to me the power to define me. Help me believe who You say I am more every day. Amen.

DAY 7

Let's Talk About Beauty

I stood in line smiling. Everyone thought I was friendly and happy. But they didn't know what was going on inside.

I watched the women around me and my thoughts spiraled, feeding off one another.

Look at her...

- Her hair is so much prettier than mine. It's so long and perfect. Mine is too blah.

- Her curves are perfect. She's thin, but still has nice breasts and backside. I curve too full in all the wrong places.

- Her eyes, chest, legs, smile. It's all better than mine.

- And I curl up further into myself wishing I could disappear because I will never be worthy of happiness and love looking like me.

Suddenly, I'm at the front of the school pickup line. I pick up my daughter and smile as we make our way out. Until someone else catches my eye, and the cycle starts all over again.

When was the last time you looked at a woman and admired her beauty without putting yourself down?

Sure, we may not say the words out loud, but in our hearts we have created a comparison trap. The minute we begin to appreciate something beautiful about someone else we are trapped in a place of criticizing ourselves.

We are meant to build one another up, not tear one another down. And when I look at another woman and judge her life based on her appearance I am not building her up. I'm using my perception of her to tear myself down. She's a footstool to get to the place I know I'll end up eventually. A place of feeling less than, not pretty enough, too big, too small, **too *me***.

Maybe we should look at one another differently.

When was the last time you looked at yourself and thought you were beautiful? Was it last week or decades ago or even never?

We've been taught that complimenting others is kind but recognizing our own beauty is vain. We've stepped into the trap that humility means belittling ourselves and putting someone else on a pedestal.

How often have I complimented someone on their hair and the automatic response is "I haven't washed it in days." It's easier to push the compliment away than to believe our hair might actually look nice.

We spend so much time frantically looking around seeing how different we are, we miss the beauty in that uniqueness.

The thing we never realize is that another person's beauty was never meant for us. I was never meant to have her eyes. You were never meant to have her legs. **You are your own kind of beautiful.**

Our worth is in our uniqueness. Maybe it's your eyes or your great hair or your smile. Maybe it's your long legs or the way your dimple is just perfectly placed. Maybe it's something you don't even see yet. But step out of the trap and look.

Your beauty is right there, a breathing fingerprint of God's creativity and love for you.

Verse: "Before I shaped you in the womb, I knew all about you. Before you saw the light of day, I had holy plans for you."
Jeremiah 1:5 (MSG)

Action Step: Look at yourself and find something beautiful. Declare it without apology today even if you have to whisper it! What is beautiful about you?

Prayer: Father, could You help me see myself the way You see me, as your beautiful daughter. I want so much to believe that I am beautiful, not in a vain way, but that I would accept the work of art you created when you made me. Let me see the beauty in my own heart and recognize it in others with abandon and without judgment. Amen.

DAY 8

I'll Have What She Has

I like home shows. I like beautiful magazine spreads with images of sparkling kitchens and cozy bedrooms. I appreciate the art of creating a beautiful space.

Chip & Joanna create so much beauty in 43 minutes. I love it. I really do.

But every time it leaves me thinking, I want a house like that.

And it takes up a little place in my mind pushing out a little bit of gratitude for what I have.

I'm not saying home shows and magazines are bad. I really do enjoy them, but this is about my heart and what happens when I see everything everyone else has that is so beautiful and perfect.

It's not just houses either. Vacations, cars, free time, appliances (yes, even appliances.) There are so many things that creep in.

Some days I feel like I am surrounded by people with more. I look around and see the house I wish I had, the car that would be so much nicer or the clothes that are always better. I never thought I was the type to try to keep up, but in my mind I seem to punish myself when I don't.

It's in magazines and store windows. Facebook posts and perfectly filtered Instagram pictures. Everywhere we look we see something more.

When I realized the neighbor's house is so much nicer than mine or the friend's vacation is so much better I struggle between being happy for them and ashamed of myself. Somehow I've bought into the idea that if I am not the best at everything then I am not worth anything.

This is where comparison gets me in trouble. I have linked my worth to other people. I have given something of mine away to people who don't even know they have it. And then I punish myself.

Am I the only one?

Maybe I am. And if that's the case, then this is all just part of my crazy mixed up brain. But if I'm not the only one, if you have ever tied your worth to the bumper of someone else's (shinier) car, then there is one thing you need to know.

God isn't comparing us.

We do that. All on our own. But the truth is that we were never meant to attach our worth to anyone but Jesus. That's it. End of story. It's not about the Joneses.

And guess what? He loves the Joneses AND us. There's no either/or. There's no score or first place trophy (or house). His love is based on who we are in Him. And before you think, *great I don't even read my Bible*, He doesn't keep a grade book for our good Christian habits or an attendance sheet for church either. It's about who we are created to be.

We create heart ties to the things we think we want or think we should be.

We get tangled up in a web of our own making, wishing for a better house or car or vacation.

We think the things we connect ourselves to on Earth is what is important.

It's really about us cutting ties that don't belong to connect with the one that does.

Verse: "No lusting after your neighbor's house—or wife or servant or maid or ox or donkey. Don't set your heart on anything that is your neighbor's."
Exodus 20:17 (MSG)

Action Step: What's one thing you can do to stop comparing? Should you take a break from home shows or travel channel? Maybe stop flipping through magazines for a bit? What is one thing that is hard for you to see someone else have? Now, make a list of things you are grateful for. Gratitude can change your whole outlook.

Prayer: Lord, sometimes it's so easy to think that the people with bigger houses or the better clothes are somehow better than me. Help me remember that You don't look at the outside or what I have. Help me to long for things that matter, things of the heart, and let go of the ways I compare myself to others. Amen.

DAY 9

So Many Circles

When it comes to people I see great big circles drawn on the ground. The circles have labels like pretty or smart or athletic. And sometimes the circles even overlap. Everyone that fits in their circle finds their place. Yet, I am left standing on the outside for one reason.

I never fit into the right circles.

It's true. I never quite fit. Not with the popular kids or the nerds. Not with the athletes or the artists. I was just there. I existed around the circles, running to see where I could fit.

I thought it would change when I grew up, but it's not much different now. The circles change names, but that's about all.

There's the popular group full of friends and activities and parties and playdates. In the church world the pastors and worship leaders fit here.

The nerdy group bent toward the philosophical or the engineering mind. Any hope of this level of intelligence went out the window with my first pregnancy.

The athletes have only changed in that they are CrossFit, runner, spinning fanatics that make me simultaneously jealous and tired (and wanting to eat a donut).

The artists are this great blend of the cool kids with real smiles and the ones always in the know of the little café or flick or music on the scene.

Sure, there are more circles, but I've never found mine.

I wonder what it would even look like.

How about "Insecure formerly smart girls who love their family and their faith but screw it all up on a regular basis?"

Is there a group for that?

I keep looking, but I never seem to find it. And most of the time I have to hide that I'm even looking. I mean you can't go around waving a sign that reads: LOOKING FOR THE MESSY PEOPLE. Because then you do fit into a circle, but that one is just called CRAZY.

What if we were never meant for circles?

If we put our worth in what circle we fit in, it will only be for part of who we are.

Circles are like Slinkys and picking one is like picking a cross section of ourselves and declaring that small piece to be all that we are, all that we'll ever be. (Because anyone who's been through high school knows you just don't up and change circles.)

So maybe I have it all wrong. Maybe high school created another false reality that became ingrained in our psyche. When I look at those circles I think of how great it would be to fit in one, but what if fitting in is actually keeping us fenced into a place we were never meant to stay forever?

Maybe if we step out of the circle we will see that the rings are invisible and we can go anywhere we are called.

Maybe we're missing the only circle that ever mattered: HIS.

Verse: "Our bodies have many parts, but the many parts make up only one body when they are all put together. So it is with the "body" of Christ."
1 Corinthians 12:12 (TLB)

Action Step: Think about this: what circles were you in during high school? Are they different now? What can you consciously do today that is outside of your circle, but in HIS?

Prayer: I am so grateful that You have this big, big circle that we all fit inside. Help me erase these circles I've drawn and move more fully in the only one that is real. The one that gives me my value and shows me unending love and grace. Thank You for loving me fully. Amen

DAY 10

It's a Stretch

I have a confession. I may have written brave when I talked about beauty, but I think my foot, or maybe my heart, is still stuck in a snare. It's a hard trap to shake, and when you've spent weeks, or years in the same place you stiffen into discomfort until you think it's normal.

I don't always believe that my worth is in my uniqueness. Instead I believe in my self — my self-worth. When we spend all our time on what feels normal sometimes we forget that it's the wrong normal. We were meant for more than comparisons and disbelief. We were meant for more than a self-image that is clouded and stuck.

I keep looking at me...myself, my life, my house, and it's so easy to see flaws. It's what I've conditioned myself to see. I've trained myself to look for the way my clothes fit too tight or the way my skin isn't flawless. I've trained myself to see your beautiful house while I only see the messy, lesser places in my own. I've trained myself to think that you will always be more and I will always be less.

I haven't flexed my faith very much. Because that's what it takes: faith. It takes faith to believe something we don't quite see. Faith to believe what God says over what we say. Faith to think something else is possible.

Maybe it's time to change perspective, even if it's a stretch.

When a muscle is not used, when it's stuck in one place for too long, we become weak. The more we use it the stronger we become.

That's easy to say when it feels good. But what about when it's hard? What about when we're so stiff we feel paralyzed?

We start small.

We stretch a little bit today.

And tomorrow we stretch a little more.

Each day matters and each day we get a little closer.

Sometimes you have to stretch to get stronger.

And we so desperately want, deep in our hearts, to be stronger. To be strong enough to believe that we are beautiful. To believe that we are worthy of God's love and all the good things He's given us here on this beautiful Earth. To believe we are worthy of salvation and good things simply because He says we are.

We want to be strong enough to believe we are worthy.

Maybe to get there we have to start by stretching.

Verse: "Truly I tell you, if you have faith as small as a mustard seed, you can say to this mountain, 'Move from here to there,' and it will move. Nothing will be impossible for you." Matthew 17:20 (NIV)

Action Step: What can you do today to stretch those stiff muscles that can't even fathom your beauty and worth? Do something small. Identify something about yourself that is good and beautiful. Recognize it by writing it down or telling a trusted friend.

Prayer: Lord, I can be so stiff in my thoughts and ideas. But You are so kind. Please come and help me stretch a little more each day, that I would become strong enough to believe what You say about me is true. Help me go beyond my old ways of thinking to a new place that believes I am worthy. Amen.

DAY 11

This May Get Uncomfortable

Unimportant, unloved, unworthy, unattractive, un, un, un.

It's a track that's on repeat and I'm tired of listening. It tells me all the things I'm lacking, all that's missing in me. It reminds me of who I think I'm not. It tells me all the things that are easier to believe because anything else would take faith.

But I'm so tired of believing lies. I'm so tired of the easy way out because it makes me feel awful. I don't want to feel this way forever.

So here's the key: I have to shut it off.

And the kicker: I will have to do it more than once.

Why? Because we gravitate toward what is familiar. We're drawn to things that we are used to, even if they are not good for us. We feel like we can't help ourselves. Our self-sabotage is our compulsion.

It's like that favorite sweatshirt in the back of my closet. It doesn't matter why I got it or where it came from, but it's perfectly worn. It's the one that I grab on a rainy day or when I'm sick. It's the one I've cried in and have slept in and wear when I really want to be comfortable. It's perfect.

Actually, it's a little too worn. It's stained and has holes. It is worn through in spots. Honestly, it's a crappy sweatshirt as far as sweatshirts go, but I keep going back to it because familiar is so comfortable.

Maybe it's time to be uncomfortable.

Nothing new will ever become comfortable if you don't use it. And not just once, but over and over again.

This idea that I am not my past. This idea that I am worthy of a future. This is uncomfortable. It looks great on a shelf, but it is so hard to wear. The only way it will get easier is to keep doing it. We hold onto what we know like a security blanket, thinking surely it is better for us than what is unknown, what feels different. We think there will never be a sweatshirt that will be as good as this one. And we hold on and hold on wondering why nothing is different.

It's like we keep reading yesterday's news because we know it so well. We know how the story goes. What to expect. What will happen. **But God never said He'd give us all the answers. He said He is the answer.**

So, let's put down the newspaper, put on that new uncomfortable sweatshirt and say, "I am worthy." Let's say it now and keep saying it until it's perfectly comfortable.

Verse: "It's impossible to please God apart from faith. And why? Because anyone who wants to approach God must believe both that he exists and that he cares enough to respond to those who seek him."
Hebrews 11:6 (MSG)

Action Step: Do you have something you need to throw away? For me, it really was a sweatshirt that kept me holding on, so I threw it away. What are you holding onto that keeps you from believing new truth? Maybe it's not a physical thing, but an emotional one. You need to let go before you can grab hold of something new.

Prayer: Lord, I am sorry for holding on to old things because they are familiar instead of trusting your truth. Help me to be comfortable with the uncomfortable, to find peace and joy in the new things you are teaching me about myself and to come to you instead of those old ideas, and give me the courage to believe the new. Amen.

DAY 12

So Many Feelings (And Worthy Isn't One)

Feelings are tricky, aren't they? There's so many swirling around and sometimes you just feel so--

Yup. Me too.

I didn't let you finish?

Just name a feeling. I promise, I've had most of them. And I'm not the only one. When I asked a group of women to complete that sentence the answers were all over the board.

- Empowered

- Poopy

- Lucky

- Resilient

- Ordinary

- Stuck

- Unmotivated

- Grateful

- Untethered

- Distracted

- Bewildered

- Blessed

I even had one woman who thoughtfully specified "Overwhelmed (negative) Grateful (positive)." (I loved that she was able to look at both sides)

Take a look at this list. How many of these feelings can you relate to? Can you say you've felt all of them? I can. And I'm sure we'll feel all of them again. The problem isn't in the feelings; the problem is in the power we give the feelings.

So often, I let my feelings take over and I'm left wishing I had done something differently. The way I yelled at the kids (for yelling, no less), the way I snapped at my husband, the way I was short with the cashier at the store. All if it can lead me down a path of thinking, of feeling. And I'm left with one idea:

If I act this way, surely I am not worthy of anything good.

There's a problem with this thinking. It means I am putting my ideas, and the assumptions I have about other's ideas, ahead of what God says about me.

I think it is time we stop fighting God.

I'm a feeler. I feel deep and often about almost anything. It's how I process the world. And I put a lot of trust in it.

We have lived with the notion that believing is a feeling. Something you wait for from the inside to propel change on the outside. But in doing this we've left out the most important aspect of believing — **faith**.

Faith is firm belief in something for which there is no proof; a complete trust. (Merriam-Webster Dictionary)

I cannot prove that I am worthy. Neither can you. This involves faith. A firm belief in all that God says about us. It's believing even when we don't see it.

We don't need to see something to believe it. We need to choose to believe and trust in the one who knows it to be true. Sometimes that's hard. Do you want to make it easier? There is a way.

(This is where Nike has it right)

Just do it.

The more we do, the easier it will get.

Let's ask for help together.

Verse: "So speak encouraging words to one another. Build up hope so you'll all be together in this, no one left out, no one left behind." I Thessalonians 5:11 (MSG)

Action Step: Right now, out loud say the following words: I am worthy. Begin to say this out loud often. Eventually, your heart will catch up. Also, think about someone you can encourage today — and do it!

Prayer: God, this feels so hard. I am trying to believe all that You say about me, but my faith is shaky and I'm searching for proof. Please help me today. Help me make the choice to believe that I am worthy. Help me to have faith that all You say about me is truth, absolute truth. Thank you. Amen.

DAY 13

Believe In Beauty

I stand in front of the mirror and sigh. The same things stare back at me and I scan each flaw wishing it away. I look at each blemish, line, and freckle. I see the circles and the shadows. But what if I could see something different?

Have you ever wondered what it would be like to believe you are beautiful? Ever wondered why you can't seem to get a handle on this whole idea? Wondered if any of it is true?

We are all created beautiful. All of us. God mentions groups of people. He talks about the teachers and the preachers, the prophets and the evangelists. Do you know what's not on that list? The pretty people. He doesn't set a group of us aside to be pretty. He doesn't classify us that way because He created us all in His image. We are all beautiful.

Beauty looks different on each of us, and maybe that's where we get hung up. We go with a consensus, some unofficial guideline of what constitutes beauty. It's as if we created a filter to judge people through, judging beauty based on these social norms. Sadly, we've even created apps for this.

But God doesn't swipe left or right when He sees our picture. He doesn't judge us based on our appearance. He loves fully. **He sees us for exactly who we are. And He likes what He sees.**

Maybe it's time we start doing the same. Maybe when we reflexively see something we don't like about ourselves (or even someone else), we should counter that by naming something we do like.

For example, when I look down at my hands I now see that I have the beginnings of old lady hands. It's true. The skin isn't as taught, there are more freckles, and no matter what I use, my skin always looks the way I imagine a hard, cracked desert floor to look. It's not my most notable flaw, but something I see all the time and think, Ugh, I have such old lady hands.

But I could change that. Not my hands, but how I see them. I can look at my hands and think how much they look like my mom's hands and her mom's hands. I can think about the joy that brings me, finding pieces of myself that so closely resemble these women I love.

Instead of saying, "I have old lady hands." And feeling lousy, I can look down and say, "I have my mom's and grandma's hands," and smile.

We always have a choice in how we see things.

Take a moment today and look in the mirror. Before you start listing your flaws, make a choice to list only things about you that are beautiful. You may not have complete faith yet, but stand there with shaky knees and allow yourself to melt. All of those hard places that feel defeated and fed up. All of those sad places that feel like you will never change. All of those angry places that ball up your fists as tight as your heart. Let them melt today.

Choose to believe in beauty today.

Choose to believe that your beauty outweighs your flaws.

Choose to believe that you are worthy.

Verse: "The Lord does not look at the things people look at. People look at the outward appearance, but the Lord looks at the heart." I Samuel 16:7 (NIV)

Action Step: Think about one thing that you like about your body. It can be like my example that is a change in perspective, or something completely separate that you can say. Now say it out loud. I have beautiful _____.

Prayer: God, help me to see my body as the beautiful creation You have made. Help me to develop a new attitude toward my body and see the beauty You embedded within, that I will live free and loved. Amen.

DAY 14

The Gift of Grace

There is a gift sitting right there in front of you. It's not your birthday. It's not Christmas. You didn't earn it, and there is only one reason you deserve it.

Go ahead. Open it. It's yours. What is it?

Grace.

The free and unmerited favor of God.

It was an ordinary day and I had gotten my friend a little something. It was nothing extraordinary, just something I had seen that made me think of her. It hadn't cost more than twenty dollars, but I knew she'd love it.

As I sat across the little table at the coffee shop, I handed her the package. Without even opening it, she said, "You shouldn't have gotten me anything." I shrugged and waited for her to open it. It was great to see her smile and I knew it was, in fact, perfect for her.

Why is it when we receive so many gifts we shake our heads? We respond with you shouldn't have or it's too much. Sometimes even I don't deserve this.

Even when it's not something wrapped in a bow how do we respond? A simple compliment: your hair looks nice or I love your shirt. This can send women squirming as they try to decide what to do with the nicety. We all know what we're supposed to do. We're supposed to say thank you. Two simple words. Yet, for most those words are anything but simple.

Asking women how they respond to compliments brings a host of replies. In my research only one person confidently said that they say thank you and feel good about it. Some women deflect with, "I got this on sale," or changing the subject. Others have an inner dialog or certain parameters for compliments.

One woman states, "If I believe them then I say thank you and I mean it. But if I don't believe them (meaning I don't agree with them) I give a smirk and say thanks and try to change the subject as quickly as possible all the while ripping apart their compliment in my head and explaining away all the reasons they can't be right."

Others reactions ranged from "pleasant embarrassment" to learning how to, or even forcing oneself to say thank you. There seems to be a spectrum of reaction and the bell curve falls far away from the intention of a compliment: to make one feel good. So many of us are trapped in this sea of undeserving, we don't know how to get to shore. We can't figure out what it looks like or how to respond. We are convinced we are undeserving.

The thing is, we're right. We, in our broken places, our weariness, our can't-seem-to-get-it-right humanity, we don't deserve it. But we are worthy of it because He made us worthy. Not because of who we are, but because of who He is. It's not about us and it's all about us at the same time.

Our only job is to say thank you.

And the best part?

If we forget, God gives anyway.

So, take hold of the gift of grace. It's for you. Every time.

Verse: "For it is by grace you have been saved, through faith—and this is not from yourselves, it is the gift of God—not by works, so that no one can boast."
Ephesians 2:8-9 (NIV)

Action Step: Say thank you. Next time someone compliments you or gives you something, just say thank you. Accept it. Make this a habit and you will learn to accept God's grace the same way.

Prayer: Lord, I long to be gracious, to accept your gifts fully and completely. Help me begin by being gracious in my life. Help me stop making excuses or brushing things off. May I be a person who accepts praise humbly, yet fully. Fully deserving, fully embracing, fully Yours. Amen.

DAY 15

You Have Gifts!

I watched her on the stage. She was funny and honest and entertaining and still full of truth. She was beautiful, but I can't get hung up on that even with her size 6 jeans perfectly tucked in her not-trying-too-hard boots. No, I couldn't get hung up on that.

She was inspiring thousands of women in a single hour. Thousands. Plus she had books. She had penned words that I think must have made their way into the hands of women all over the world.

She was walking in her giftings. The same giftings I wanted. I wanted the looks (yes, I still get stuck there sometimes), but more than that I wanted the success. I rationalized it as being for God, so it must be ok. I wanted to inspire women that way. I want. I want. I want. Now I sound like my kids did when they were toddlers. Sometimes I'm pretty sure I'm a toddler in God's eyes.

Not wanting something and not having it are two different things.

I've spent my life wanting. Wanting to be more: to be prettier, smarter, funnier, sexier, friendlier, better. I've built my life staring want in the face trying to shake it until I get the things I think I'm looking for.

The problem is that I've been so busy wanting I did not consider having.

There are silent places deep within, hidden behind the daily smiles and I'm fine responses. Those places don't multitask. If I'm so busy thinking about the things I want to be, there is no room for considering what I am.

The want takes the spotlight and what I have is left in the shadows.

But what if we changed that? What if we were able to look at ourselves and recognize all that we have? Not the things we have but the gifts that make us who we are. What if we moved the spotlight?

Instead of saying I have no gifts, what if you could say I am a great leader or I am really good at teaching?

Sound prideful? I thought so, too. But then I realized that God gave me gifts. He gave you gifts. These are the unique things that He wove into the fibers of who we are to make us the perfect thread for our part of this amazing tapestry He's created.

When we deny the gifts God has given us, we reject God as an artist, we reject our potential, and we reject the ways in which we affect others.

It's time to stop saying we have no gifts. It's time to move the spotlight and recognize those intricate strengths and abilities that are uniquely ours so we can be part of something beautiful.

Verse: "We have different gifts, according to the grace given to each of us. If your gift is prophesying, then prophesy in accordance with your faith; if it is serving, then serve; if it is teaching, then teach; if it is to encourage, then give encouragement; if it is giving, then give generously; if it is to lead, do it diligently; if it is to show mercy, do it cheerfully."
Romans 12:6-8 (NIV)

Action Step: Write down one of the gifts God has given you. Maybe you're a great listener or excel in organization. Maybe it's your patience with your kids or the way you worship. Be real and honest. I dare you to write down 3 things!

Prayer: Thank you for giving me gifts. Not just the things you give me, but the things You created in me. Help me see them as beautiful, fully recognizing each gift as something special. Help me not dismiss things that You see as beautiful. Amen.

DAY 16

Identifying Your Gifts

Sometimes it is not enough to say something is there. You have to take the time to really see it before it matters.

If we admit that we have gifts, strengths and abilities, but stop there, we are missing the point. This is where the threshold of pride comes into place because we are so busy looking at ourselves. We don't think about what to do beyond that.

We need to recognize that God gave us these talents, not because we are worthy in our own strength, but because He made us worthy. His gifts to us came at higher price than many of us will ever know, yet He gives without hesitation. There is no second-guessing, sticker shock, it's the thought that counts mentality. He has given each of us unique gifts and abilities.

Now the ball is in our court.

We've talked a lot about the unique gifts God gives each of us. But sometimes everything feels uncertain and cloudy like we are looking at life through the wrong glasses.

Here are a few resources I've found that help identify your gifts and abilities.

Spiritual Gifts Assessment Tools[1] — This is a fantastic article by Lifeway with tools you can utilize to help you identify your areas of spiritual gifts. Take your time on this one and see what it means for you.

We Can[2] — A short blog article that has a strong biblical base to help you think about your strengths. A quick read that you won't regret.

Personality Type Test[3] — This is an online test that is similar to the Myers-Briggs

Personality Indicator. Although, shorter and less precise, it will still help you recognize how you are wired and how that relates to you and the world around you. The site gives a great summary that I found insightful. If you want more detailed information you can look for information about the official Myers Briggs Personality Indicator.

These resources are a great start to understanding more about who you were created to be and how to apply that to your life. Remember you are worthy. Believe it today.

Verse: "Use whatever gift you have received to serve others, as faithful stewards of God's grace in its various forms. If anyone speaks, they should do so as one who speaks the very words of God. If anyone serves, they should do so with the strength God provides, so that in all things God may be praised through Jesus Christ. To him be the glory and the power for ever and ever." 1 Peter 4:10-11 (NIV)

Action Step: Complete one of the resources above and make note of a few gifts that are part of the fabric of who you are. These ideas are a great springboard for believing who God made you to be.

Prayer: Lord, this feels scary. It's easier to look at my flaws than it is to look at my gifts. But I choose to believe that you have put good things in me. Help me be brave enough to explore them with an open heart. Amen.

DAY 17

Start Small

Yesterday, my husband ran to the store after a snowstorm. I was making chili and had no cornbread. The roads were clear, so he went on his way.

A little while later I heard the door open and close behind me. Grateful he was home safe (and with cornbread) I thanked him while I finished something at the computer. A moment later a bouquet of flowers was laid on my desk.

It was little. Simple. But it made my day.

What things show you that someone loves you? Is it even about things?

Of course not! We're all quick to reply. But there is a truth in the beauty of gifts given to you by someone who loves you. There's a tenderness. A reminder that you are loved so much that someone would invest in you. Money. Time. Thought. You are worthy of that investment.

It wasn't the flowers so much as the fact that he thought of me. When he was schlepping through snow and at the store he thought of me and wanted to make me smile.

In life, sometimes we forget to invest in people. Sometimes we wish someone would invest in us. Today isn't about wishing. It isn't about doing enough. Today I would encourage you to do one thing.

- Do something for yourself.

- Buy flowers. Just for you because they are beautiful.

- Cook the dinner you love for no other reason than you love it.

- Get your nails done because you want to.

- Go for a walk somewhere beautiful.

- Listen to the song you love, over and over again.

- Wear that dress because it makes you feel good.

- I love butternut squash soup. No one else in my family does. Guess how often I made butternut squash soup in my house. Never.

I had figured since no one else would eat it, it wasn't worth making. Somehow I had decided that I wasn't worthy of something I love just because no one else validated it. **You are worthy of enjoying things you love, even if no one else does.**

The point today is not what you do. It's just taking a moment to do something for yourself because you are worthy of love and beauty.

Verse: "This is why I remind you to fan into flames the spiritual gift God gave you" 2 Timothy 1:6 (NLT)

Action Step: What's something you love? Even if no one else does, do that today. See how much joy it brings and how it reminds you that you are worthy of enjoying the good things God has for you in life.

Prayer: Lord, help me feel bold enough to seek out and make time for things that bring me joy. I want to believe that I am worthy of experiencing things that are beautiful. Thank you for all the gifts You give. Help me experience them fully. Amen.

DAY 18

It's the Little Things

I got in the car and started driving. I had a list of things to do, places to go with three kids in tow. Most of the list I'd rather not do, but the kids kept saying we had no food in the house (I think it was just the absence of cereal that worried them). Before I could do any of it, I remembered needing gas.

I hate pumping gas. It's a little thing. Really. It takes a few minutes. I know. But I rank it somewhere between taking out the garbage and vacuuming the car.

As I drove, I glanced at the gauge and saw that my tank was, in fact, full. Right then I smiled because I knew. He did it. My husband must have filled up my car yesterday when he was out. For me.

Sometimes it's the little things that become the big things.

Little things in life that show love. Little things that make us feel loved. Sometimes these add up to more than grand gestures. Why? Because they are so personal.

Someone filling your gas tank may not be the thing that makes a difference to you. But for me, it showed love.

Even in the Bible, between all the grand gestures, the burning bush and the empty tomb, God blesses people in little ways that matter to them.

- He gives flour and oil that never runs out. (I Kings 17:7-16)

- He gave personal experience in the middle of a crowd. (Luke 8:40-48)

- He provided wine for a celebration. (John 2:1-11)

God cares about the little details as much as He cares about the big ones. He longs to bless you intimately in the unique way that you need Him to show up. It's far less about the act, and more about how well He knows your heart.

Verse: "Every good and perfect gift is from above, coming down from the Father of the heavenly lights, who does not change like shifting shadows." James 1:17 (NIV)

Action Steps: Read the Bible stories above and look at how God provides so personally for these people. Look for Him and all the little things He does for you to show His love in real ways every day.

Go beyond that and do something little for someone in your life. The size of the gift matters less than the size of the heart.

Prayer: Lord, I long to see the little ways You bless me. Help me not look over the many things You do for me every day, but to see these things as reminders of how intimately You know me. Help me be a blessing to others in the same way, that they would recognize more of Your love for them. Amen.

DAY 19

Value in the Unseen

How many items are in your house? 100? 1000? 10,000? Too many to count? How about just in your kitchen or your dresser?

I have a drawer in my nightstand. I keep some journals and a few special things in there. I have spent less and less time with those treasures lately, and the drawer showed it.

When I finally decided it was time to clean it out I found old batteries mixed with old love notes, old pictures mixed with old receipts. Cleaning it out only took fifteen minutes or so, and as I did I found socks.

Now, before you start thinking *more junk that doesn't belong*, these were not just any socks. They were a first pair of socks for my oldest daughter. Their smallness took my breath and I held them reveling in twelve years of yesterdays.

Those socks may be just a thing, but to me they were a reminder of a person, a feeling, a time.

Our lives are full of things: drawers stuffed with hope in all that we can touch. As if the ability to wrap our fingers around something makes it valuable.

Those socks were no more valuable than the dead batteries, but to me they brought back memories of the things that really mattered.

We collect and store and buy to have all we need, but would you rather have everything you necd for five minutes or for a lifetime?

The value of something is not in our ability to touch it, rather in our inability. If I put my worth in all that I have, I will never be worth enough. We are more than the things we fill our home with. We are more than the objects we cushion our lives with. We are about all that is unseen.

Love

Joy

Breath

Grace

Faith

It's time we stop putting all our eggs in that basket we just had to have. The eggs and the basket are just more things. We are worth more than the things that surround us. It just depends on where we put our hope.

Verse: "Take delight in the LORD, and he will give you the desires of your heart." Psalm 37:4 (NIV)

Action Step: Find something you treasure. Yes, an object. Now think about what it is you really value about it. Does it remind you of a special time or a special person? Was it something you worked hard for or nearly lost? Think about the bigger picture of why you value it. God looks at you with even more fondness and value.

Prayer: I want so much to believe in how You see me, God. I want to believe in my value, my worth, not because of what I am on the outside or what I do in this world, but because of who You made me to be and how very much You love me. Amen.

DAY 20

Too Much and Not Enough

I walked away from the conversation knowing I had just messed it all up. I had been talking to a new friend at my daughter's school. We were getting to know one another and making small talk about the kids. It was going well, and I even made a mental note — *I could really see us becoming good friends!* I tried not to smile like a crazy person. I may have failed.

We kept talking and I began to feel excited, surprised even, that this person liked me. It felt great. I was already picturing summer barbeques and winter sledding with her and her family. I didn't say that of course. But I must have hinted at something stronger than the just met you and getting to know you level because her expression changed. The warm smile that had been there was replaced with slightly raised brows and a fake smile nodding agreement with a barely noticeable hesitation.

And I realized I'd done it again. Too much. I was too much.

There is a very thin line that exists between being noticed and fitting in.

I've spent my life wanting to be the best, smartest, and (in all honesty) the most beautiful woman to ever exist. Yes. It's true. I'm not proud of this, but it is the truth.

But long before my conversation at the school there was a part of me that knew that when you are too much, it's not a good thing. I was too emotional, too black and white, too honest. **When the world says you are too much you become less of yourself. Eventually, you are not really sure who you are.**

So I stood on this thin line of too much and not enough. The simultaneous desire to be more and less. I spent my life on a tightrope and I was exhausted.

But what if I stopped following the line?

What if I decided to just be me?

In all of my imperfection?

In all of my mistakes?

In all of the things I do right? (Yes, we can admit when we do something right.)

When we stare at the ground following some invisible line, we can only see our feet.

I think it's time we looked up.

Maybe if we stepped off the line and looked around us we would see that we're all just walking around on our tiptoes, eyes fixed on the ground. There never was a line or a rope. Just us, creating this act based on assumed expectations.

It's time to stop losing yourself in an effort to please everyone else.

The truest form of you is exactly what God created you for. The world needs you, not a tightrope walker.

Verse: "Oh yes, you shaped me first inside, then out; you formed me in my mother's womb. I thank you, High God— you're breathtaking! Body and soul, I am marvelously made! I worship in adoration—what a creation! You know me inside and out, you know every bone in my body; You know exactly how I was made, bit by bit, how I was sculpted from nothing into something. Like an open book, you watched me grow from conception to birth; all the stages of my life were spread out before you, the days of my life all prepared before I'd even lived one day." Psalm 139:13-16 (MSG)

Action Step: What is something you haven't done because you thought it was too much, thought it would make you look silly, or thought no one would understand? Find something that brings you joy and step off the line and do that thing. Be you, even if it feels like you're too much.

Prayer: Lord, I trust that you made me who I am for a reason. You placed desires and characteristics in my heart. Help me stop measuring who I think I should be based on how others will see me, and instead step forward in courage to be fully who you created. Amen.

FINAL NOTE

For You

The last 20 days have been full of looking at how worthy you are. In recognizing the innate beauty of who you are and embracing it, you experience freedom.

But there is a hard truth that you should know. One day, it will happen that you, even in all of your worthiness, cannot do it alone.

You won't be enough. Sometimes life will be too much, too hard. The ground may shake beneath you and you may be scared and unsure.

This just means we are human. We've spent this time learning to believe that we are worthy, but do not mistake that with who we are. ***Our worth does not mean we are God. It means we are valued by God.***

When we are able to look at our weakness, our inability, without it affecting how we view our worth, then we have truly come to a place of trusting God in all that we are.

Believe you are worthy. In the hard times. In the times when you fail. In the times when you are scared. You are worthy.

It won't always be easy, but good things rarely are. This is not the end of a journey. ***This is your beginning.***

I am so grateful you came on this journey with me. Maybe you got through it in 20 days, maybe it took longer. Either way we are both here now, closer to understanding who we are because of who God is.

* * * * *

I would love to hear how Worthy has changed the way you think about your worth. Send me an email at becky@myinkdance.com. I'd love to pray for you specifically, plus hearing from readers makes my day!

Prayer: Lord, thank you for showing me who I am in You. I long to believe Your truths and walk in them fully everyday knowing that I am worthy. I am worthy to be called your child. I am worthy of love and joy and goodness. Nothing that I do can change my value. Thank you for the grace I need to move forward in this new thinking, this new believing. You are a good God and I am your child. Thank you for loving me fully, always. Amen.

ACKNOWLEDGEMENTS

Thank You is Not Enough

I'm finding these words the most difficult to write because words fail to show the depth of gratitude for the people who helped make this book possible. I may have strung the words, but God gave them meaning and my people held the string.

Andrew, you always believe in me more than I believe in myself. You have supported my dreams and given me more than I could have asked for. Thank you for loving me so well. Nineteen years is just the beginning.

Eliza, Timmy and Anna, your very existence inspires me to write words of hope. I long for you to live life fully believing who you are in Christ. Thank you for always encouraging me and saying that I am a writer long before I was able to.

Mom and Dad, you built a foundation of love in my life that I stand on every day. You always said I could reach the stars. You made that possible.

Natalie and Samantha, your encouragement and help made these words what they are today. Thank you for your editing and for your friendship.

All the women who shared their stories, thank you for trusting me with your truth.

To all those who have been part of my journey, thank you will never be enough.

RESOURCES

Spiritual Gift Assessments

1. Spiritual Gift Assessment Tools:
   http://www.lifeway.com/Article/Wo
   men-Leadership-Spiritual-gifts-
   growth-service

2. We Can Article:
   https://bitesizebiblestudy.blogspot.
   com/2014/06/we-can.html

3. 16 Personalities Test:
   https://www.16personalities.com/fr
   ee-personality-test

ABOUT THE AUTHOR

Rebecca Hastings

Rebecca believes in embracing grace in the messy real of life. She captures hard, uncomfortable, often unspoken feelings and brings light, honesty and God's truth to them in a relatable way.

A wife and mother of three in Connecticut she writes imperfect finding faith along the way.

Visit her blog, My Ink Dance, for more extraordinary grace in ordinary life.